letting go

of who i was:

Chronicle Poetry

Daniel S. Sandorf

ISBN: 979-8-218-37830-1
Dan's Inner Narrative
Front cover image by Daniel S. Sandorf
Book design by Daniel S. Sandorf
First printing edition 2024.
Dansinnernarrative.com

From: childhood.

For: healing.

To: moving on…

An emotion forgotten.
A bleary moment folded.
A shivering question soaring.
An instant regret devoted.

- Dan

the foundation

…

hidden narratives

injured poems / 152-162

the foundation

memo of negativity

when thinking
life had
no more
pure perfection,
the realization became
more so survival
when there was this aspect,
the whole direction
of the
entire world
felt imaginative.
beginning
to realize,

. . .

understanding-
inspired more
than not-
often most things
start to
become heavily hellish.
so is time
merely just
a concealment
to experience
the bottomless pit?

falling

so feeling stigmatized
compares to delicately
cutting this thin rope.
holding in my hand
and measuring
every change.
even so rationalizing,
even fictionalizing
for justifying
every conversation.
for so long in continued time,
i pretended long ago-

…

in the wake of every voice…
what i was pursuing
became earnestly clear
to follow every voice that i hear
to pour sense into senseless
stimulation.
since when is expecting danger
already immature?
to believe with judgment,
i am existing too early, already.

vulnerability

suffocating underwater.
swimming right below,
then picturing myself
right below the sea.
haunting myself
by swimming
right below
an infinite
feet of water.
holding my breath,
seeing where life would-
and so could
and take me

…

just a few feet
right below.
only five feet-
became twelve feet.
because during a time
at my truest self-
in my most
heartwarming self,
floating when the sun
would- and
so could melt.

…

and melt,
and blend right below
with the water
to open my eyes
to the world-
with this world
from the
excruciating reflection
bouncing back
right below
the water.

nothing inside

the most alone emotions
depicted of engraved
meanings
on my bedroom wall
were these thoughts
of penetrating danger.
who was on the other side?
my window *was tapping*
little pebbles.
pounding just about
my window
was kidnapping
natural light-
laying on every surface
full of the closest-

. . .

close to my wholesome
memories for emptying
my head from a day
out into the world-
in one day.
so how?
so even… possibly
strictly even handmake
an entire dialogue inside
from outside,
creating a lasting impact
tumbling, perhaps
crafting emptiness

...

staring at completely nothing,
reconnecting the utmost
of something,
completely empty
for stealing the joy
of a wonderland.

character development

i felt everything
at a younger age.
everything was close
to my heart.
i felt my heart
beating and beating
until it stopped.
i wasn't any different
than a zebra
with an extra stripe,
sometimes.
but because sensitively,

…

i felt rare to live,
where was the air
i intensely inspired
from the present
to extremely let out
in the past
when i didn't
put a second thought…
was i wasting
time on this earth?
because why was my mind
playing a game
of pick-up sticks.

...

and i see how they drop.
they are scattered.
the right stick
will create pressure,
for the wrong move
is easier to see than finding
the right answer,
sometimes.
was i falling
into a dark episode?
turning on countless lights
until i get confused?

. . .

or do i get stuck?
with the repeated circle?
it got faster
with every *roundabout.*
turning off countless lights,
every little scenario
i played in the dark,
while playing hide and seek forever,
it was truly a dark place.
maybe i was never any different.
so flipping this card over,
i could think
of the next move.
using how i thought

…

i was never loved.
for watching
how my own shadow
is not twisting and turning
compared to everyone else.
but still, owning
every defense,
as a child,
i cannot take away
how i felt
and how i thought.
and even everyone
has hidden drawers-

...

way down beneath.
opening them
was in a pretty dark place, too.

accepting

i wish
i could've traveled
a million miles away.
being as a balloon
losing air,
i wish i didn't know
where ending up
the safest alone
from falling behind?
wishing to wander
a sense of comfort
from falling behind.
never believing…

…

i could’ve
been the leader?
yet where was my faith?
passed around,
waiting on the times
i was deemed too “slow”
during the times-
i could’ve
spoken up
because i didn't know.

questions still remain

each footstep
felt tampered with.
my thought process
encountered
upon someone else-
for owning up
to my biggest fears,
living with the fear
of constantly falling.
constantly with
the fullness
of this suspicion.

. . .

the consistent fear
was acting so deranged
to pressure my mind-
on existence.
for unwillingly
unscrewing
every little detail
that i was actually
never meant to be here.
even so,
for remembering
surrounding myself
as a failure

…

actually taught
that i was invisible.
though, on that thought
i hated myself
even more.

looking back

often, i feel detached
from my own values
for standing above
my own height.
often, i see that i am
just pressing down on myself.
acting out an immediate reaction
for understanding the bottom line
of each stage in my life…
through what is carried out
to be- apparently
so short lived
in other people's eyes.

…

often, i feel trapped
in the past.
but i see now how active
the lightheartedness
of fire can actually be.
for struggling
with something,
i blamed the past…
so sunk for how
i saw something
so rooted and observed by.
in a sense of something
so smooth accomplished by.

if perfectionism existed

this is for cherishing
and fulfilling the thought
of everything
this known symmetry
was inflicted upon me.
for bending every reflection
of myself for just knowing
something.
so truly convinced,
truly, i was brought up
understanding
in a distorted way.

…

emotionally influencing
the *perfect* strategy.
reinforcing these open doors,
my inner voices
wanted to damage
every *riotous feeling,*
for acting upon
these fighting thoughts,
creating a louder atmosphere
of each hollow step,

…

realizing untaught interest
because my inner life
became more
so more tasteless.
bringing more awareness
was knowing definition
of an asymmetrical process.

little darker thoughts

why can't determining
the difference between
voicing comfortably
and continually
walking away from…?
determining the entirety
of hushing quiet.
walking away
from forcefully
forgetting the grave
of my existence-

…

even when wanting
to say, truthfully,
i rarely felt right
just standing here.
savoring the need-
even to hang on
the need-
to even exist
from every little thing
my childhood
could just set out.
seeing what drove deep
down- for me to be.

...

i was going
to change this word?
so tasting the little idea
spun drastically.
having any sense
of "originality"?
one day though,
truthfully-
those long days
played a loop
of these continuous
thunderstorms.
losing motivation-

...

drove deep down
as intimidating fear
for not feeling okay.
for continuously
rattling every bone
of mine close by.
so truthfully,
when will i feel
okay again?

shower and sprinkle

trying and
alleviating
treating myself,
blending in everywhere
from every single image.
experiencing my childhood
through a blank canvas,
i wanted to violently
throw paint- in a way
for encountering every little
emotion-
and explore how it was.

...

so can it be illegal
to just rewrite it?
when every changing
perspective
caused a surprising amount
of no tenderness.
i was suppressing-
to a point where
i was repressing
a whole new narrative.
when surrounding myself
in the untruthful water
of every steppingstone.

…

i felt the water…
just stretching the history.
occupying these memories.
standing by every surface…
to just sink
because hopefully
every stepping stone
erodes a path-
hopefully
burning a path-
to childbirth.

powerful thinking

why was it lonely
to be on a street-
where both ways
was a dead end?
for listening
to the voices
on my shoulders
dressed in
absolute pressure
to say the most
absurd things
in the heat of a moment.

…

it was so exhilarating
to be influenced-
right or wrong…
it was a difficult decision.
because i see all around me…
not looking both ways
when crossing the road.
it was exhilarating-
nowhere that i can see
since a weapon can be
used anywhere.

…

absorbing an intimate response
how the moon can fall right
out of the sky,
still illuminating…
i hugged the moon.
absorbing its every piece of light.
just when being alone,
getting robbed felt,
always a guarantee.
so in the name
of a dragonfly,
how can i learn
to breathe fire?

...

but also, how can i
learn to fly?
when needing great clarity or
wisdom.
searching for guidance
from any mythical creature-
or any sort of breathing soul.

sprouting wings

i want to make my way
into this world.
so what was
i meant for?
why was i brought here?
i want to be *somebody.*
sincerely, as a child
being a *somebody*
was a faint dream of mine.
awakening a forceful nature
breathing in nature-
from the tallest of trees, ever.

. . .

and be not- not afraid at all.
falling at all, ever
from a great distance.
for constantly noticing
the summer rain
has already started.
so what does a tree
become when sawed off?
a broken perception.
since it means
a new life can sprout
somewhere else.

something special

why are my differences
any different than being
unmatched?
from taking the standpoint
of being *"unique"*
shaping a life-
casting someone else
to be a star.
for going up
and landing on the moon.

...

from a position
where anything-
can be dreamed of.
reflecting upon a portion
of child-like wonder.
my mind- was enchanted.
inventing a certain existence
was sacred
in absorbing…
every creative thought
to aspire a true closeness
within myself.

growing creative

flying fearless
the world enough
was already ~~mine.~~
and these wings
on my shoulders
became a mind
of its own.
gravitating towards
new land-
covered with secrets.
creating new meanings
of riskless and recklessness.

...

so water filled-
had filled up
my brain- and clouded
my eyes.
still, i was seeing
underwater?
my armor
became unbreakable.
suddenly dropping,
reaching the runway.
exactly, what was
to crumble me?

...

building this world
inside my hands-
feeling the power
to take it all away.
a castle crushed
in between the sands
within the palm
of my hands,
a piece of paper,
with every crumbled piece
i just couldn't see.

…

every fold flew
careless along
the wind.
a paper airplane.
or even…
simple creative ideations.
empty sprite soda cans.
pretending it flew
on a sunny day.

new land

growing wings
was supposed
to be special.
flying up,
up as high-
and up as possible.
i was having the chance,
swimming in every cloud
from the air's resistance.
hiding behind every facade
when every person
i see… doesn't
even know who i am.

...

learning a bird's eye view
was actually small to me.
high altitude, already
was nothing new to me.
and being stripped,
was i scared?
becoming
someone new?
falling down,
i must've been shaken,
causing a natural disaster
with everyone around me.
forever scared at the time
from feeling confused

...

from making a mistake.
learning, falling,
when being stuck
in the ocean.
sinking within the sound
of rain, i kept on floating.

do i believe?

when believing
the power
of everything,
holding
the very quietness
of my world,
i felt the power
of everything.
believing when
holding onto
a stereotypical wand
of a shining star.

…

instead, only
with my imagination
it was anything
i had imagined it to be.
but in my actual head,
it was the awareness
of how my sight…
eventually grew… darker.
sitting on a throne
holding a helping hand,
was i blindly sitting
on top of any planet,
waiting and wearing
any sort of crown?

viewing new adventures

i was having a conversation
and i wasn't there.
but from a watch tower-
overlooking new land,
and becoming silent,
it was a cloudless day.
so feeling vulnerable
this sort of lift
was unlike anything else.
this sort of lift drove me up,
climbing on imaginary vines
from out of this world
when hardly holding on.

…

waiting on this sort of lift
was throwing me out
unto a raft
or unto space.
not needing a paddle…
or a spaceship.
instead, drifting in a direction
not needing the afraid-ness
of drowning from each kick
in a swim- like motion.
and trail where i haven't
gone before
in search of any planet.

...

burning a passion
to lay in the sun
when feeding myself
to the sharks,
i can finally
touch the stars.

just waiting…

the start of a new day…
skyrocketing
just as the sun
was settling beneath
the reflective water.
it is easier said
for searching
in any outlook
of genuine fear
from hearing
any predatory noise
for straightforwardly…

...

casually- walking
straight through
into danger,
into the heavy fog.
stepping in closer
and creating the atmosphere,
the only person standing
on a late October night,
telling tales on October 31st,
i didn't even scare myself.

...

every street corner,
the streetlights
weren't visible anymore:
practically invisible.
the fog had misted.
i became comforting
the behavior
where no one
had to know
my pure existence.
becoming out of sight
in plain existence.

limitless views

sitting only, sitting forever.
sleeping three hundred,
four hundred million
years again, covered
in a fully unzipped
sleeping bag.
sitting alone-
i started to believe
that i hung the stars.
i actually believed
i hung the moon
and the sun.

…

making up
a warm blanket
suddenly now
i'm paired well
with a straight jacket
around- feeling safe?
soon revealing a castle
as grand as an
evergreen forest.
the answer followed
a river straight down
a waterfall- and if following it…
more likely- being pushed in
was sounding out
the right answer.

. . .

so this timer
set out of nowhere,
had set off
a burnt crunch
for the castle
fitting my image-
had every threat
locked on me.

overthinking

noticing a tree's shadow
observing unattractiveness,
the surroundings
felt harbored by the stars
falling asleep.
so dreaming- everything
can seem… so still.
so imagining breathing
underneath the water-
skipping each building,
my legs- just couldn't stop
living high spirited
through the night.

…

originating a royal
symphony,
everything seemed
so grand inside
my head.
imagining every
pulled string,
crafting the
slightest change.

isolated home

what age held this
imagination
when noticing the calm
before a storm?
holding the sky-
and creating
a scenario,
fictionalizing the sky-
during the right
exact moment…
of telling the right
exact moment
of a story:

...

how the wind
can carry a current.
and lift the earth
right- out of my hands.
for a second- drowning
out of water- suffocating
a sense of breathlessness
because it was sweltering
from just cheerlessly melting-
because of a stitched-up wound.

…

the storm started,
covered in this area,
the shivering coldness
of a wet blanket
threw darkness
hues, royal blue-
a sweet purple,
on a beaming
sunset orange.

…

lightning strikes
are atomic-
and the clouds
resembled
a drenched
protection.

peaceful sense

i wish-
i was
somewhere else.
honestly, acting free
in an unfinished house.
it was my own
vibrant open world.
filled with a pixelated life.
sinking during a time
on a touch for realism.
slowly slipping for a time

…

i wish
i was-
somewhere else.
at least in my own world,
at the time…
i just belonged
with my own sense
of security for my creativity
where my *"differences"*
didn't have to define me.
during any time,

. . .

roaming with
an imaginative idea-
i sat on backwards,
my head.
giving myself a new life.
my world was lit up
with the many doors,
opening blindly.
i wish-
i was
never afraid
to walk in…
to an uncompleted
house.

formative times

i wish
i had a superpower.
the intensity
of living forever.
for time to be standing still.
childhood should appear…
to be magical.
having something-
maybe everything
last forever.
having an honest
point of view
so warmly precious.

...

living in a moment
and wandering
if a cliff- was the edge
of the world?
having *"vivid imagination"*
from composing
these worlds,
an entire universe,
i gratefully strung.
living in each scenario
was admirable.
my imagination formed
a spectacle on the world.

fearfulness

so sure
i was held behind-
from a sinister soul-
a sinister intuitiveness.
i felt the broken child…
going against
my intuitiveness
and forgetting
a pretty world.
feeling so special
from building up
such suspense.

...

counting each day,
i needed to go back
to where it all fell enough
during the pitch black.
soaring on a swing,
the air dropped
in my stomach.
gripping my fingers,
a fiery combustion...
traveling.
but not until
i let go.

...

and i did.
i let go.
feeling this felt
endlessly long ago.
it all seemed
the broken child
was walking
with an overflow
state of mind
with his one strange
wolf pack.

...

he kept his tail
between his legs
as he saw
in his field of vision,
the full moon
when everyone else
howled in tune.
The Fearful Night Sky,
the one painted picture
was fearfulness.

haunting relationship

how am i supposed to heal?
asking for forgiveness
to exactly pinpoint
if forgiving…
do they know?
if asking for forgiveness
is on their radar.
so step by step
what is the definition
of forgiveness?

...

choosing a grotesque
form of regret?
or a reflection?
from cultivating
this detailed mirror.
every imperfection
wasn't ever good enough.
because every slap mark
created a scar.
lingering when two enemies
suffer from secret history.
did it take a day
or even a week?

…

perhaps, years later
your presence
was never the same.
so how come cowering
at every remark,
i was at least trying?
is it escaping?
trying to move on.
because when two
opposite magnets
became attracted

...

by forcing
how my own
self-worth
was put on you.
seemingly controlled
by every little emotion-
even unprovoked,
the eggshells
just break louder
the more
i am around you.

left in the pouring rain

truly, i felt shaken.
i was trying
and i felt dazed…
eternally trying,
finding my way home.
reminiscing about my scent.
i found a directionless map,
and fascination progressed
this anticipation, i had lost
hollow distance even more.
time turned very quickly.
time was a shot in the dark-
awaiting the first day,

. . .

the street was flooding,
flourishing,
this bouquet of rain
had asked the little duckling,
how homely?
traveling along the gutter
basked in the rain.
the heaviness
daringly fell
in front of me?
so each drop
felt somehow
fragmentary?

…

i cannot remember
my reaction
of lightning flashing,
quickly imprinting
from every angle,
a camera had flashed
in front of me?
are my clothes
going against
my favor?
i'm drenched
from the rain
of the sound
of lava flowing
along my journey.

...

the countless pavements
felt miles and miles away,
an infinite number
painted monochrome
from the foreverness.
the cloudiness
followed stronger
and stronger.

imaginary mind games

what memory
was staying circling sane?
working for amazed individuals
carving into specific rock.
mining any rare element.
diamonds i had in mind.
replaying this insane picture:
how i could've created
each rare element,
each rare moment
as i felt someone
along with me.
instructing every
tough thought.

...

falling in seriously
boiling volcanoes.
sinking- and burning
every hurtful thing
that i could've ever said.
lingering into the atmosphere,
overpowering a reaction
from something so empowering,
i set the time of day.
so what memory can shatter
natural wonder?
a memory played in slow motion
during a stop motion picture.

…

every movement…
a rare moment
has proven meaning…
solely- a raw purpose.
in fact- why was it painful
having new meaning
for everything?

certain deepness

the stairs
i stood on,
i thought
the steepness
was my natural
born enemy.
always an element
indestructible,
for this gravity
i never felt
the same.

...

so feeling different-

and still,

somehow

i wanted

to be the same.

because

the moment

developing

recollection

i knew something

was off.

…

so while taking
a focused
emotional breath
from more
than two unhealed
emotional wounds,
i was brought
into this world.
and already *certain,*
already i was
unwanted.

left alone moments

holding onto
a suitcase full
of rocks,
my backpack
felt weighted
to full heartedly
remember-
what is even
worth remembering?
the small
achy moments?

...

suddenly intruding
holding in
from an intrusive
thought?
holding onto
my own grudge
from remembering
the minor details,
for remembering
this precise minute?
and sporadically
remembering
the minor details.

...

but forgetting
my existence
was someone
else's big picture
on the world
where i was clueless
on the world outside.
simply walking outside,
so concentrated
on the world outside.
the entire world had a life?

...

where am i living exactly?
when growing
in any which direction
felt frightening.
remembering-
where was i looking?

hidden narratives

i dream, hopeless

maybe, i have lost
an entire paragraph
of words.
hurting- meaning,
i dream.
giving up the reason
for a calling,
i embodied the kid
i wish
i was still
simple minded
during a time-

. . .

i played pointlessly
unavoidably,
i dream.
a splash
of colder water
was supposedly reality.
so accidental anything.
the power
i lost,
i found.

…

finding accidental,
astronomical
spacious room
of the universe,
i dream.

out there

is there such a thing
of the end of the world?
for flying in front
of an invisible wall,
if the universe
can still dream?
drawing near, unique-
understanding
more alike than we think.
i'd rather spend
my extra lost memories
during my lonely time
from a true loss.

…

from a cry,
how do we express
in the many ways
even so possible
what we feel.
i, only, ever
was crying-
inwardly for help.
for something only
ever so down
in front of me.
seeing the whole sky
in front of me.

…

i wanted at the time
to only, ever think, carefree.
granted, looking down,
reasoning i was a nobody
to some degree…
in the water
of the infinity pool
i was swimming in

misunderstanding

something in my head
was telling me
i am just off.
better explaining
that sliding down a swirl
where likely being put
on a different whirl,
it was so different
in this world.
so was it some sort
of magic losing sight of?

…

i couldn't just pick at
from the world, where
in a super-secret cave
i learned.
truly concerned,
held in meaning
of the darkness
i burned.
truly learning darkness
of what was returned.

...

a secret
i held in
from keeping the vicinity
of my life
from countless worries.
i shut myself down
from knowing,
knowing capable love.

slasher films

and openly seeking
who had the knife?
as i stand behind
with myself,
grinning dreadful
somewhere,
openly hiding,
i was anywhere
in real life.
possibly, maybe,
even somewhere
in the in-between
divine, floating
in the afterlife.

…

how i'm sure.
so emotional.
at least over there…
i fell mad, dancing
with the total eclipse.
somehow, flipping over
a sly note.
turning the page,
i was left rewriting
the scripts
as a mastermind.

...

cluding that
i uncovered the potion,
that i am at least
forged somewhere
by the elixir of life.
but openly
i still had the knife.
believing in the supernatural,
i had a certain devotion
to entangle the very potion
of eternal life.

…

stealing someone
else's sacred land,
i was now exiled.
and i caught onto
myself, continuing
a path, continuing wild.
coming to life,
i still held onto the knife.
piercing what i
exactly perceived
as far as the knife went in.
as i retrieved.

...

how can i stay true
with the older purpose's
i once had in my life?
exactly, which version
of myself had the very knife?

getting there

to know this feeling,
sinking certain pain.
struggling
for a broken dream
was never going
to be sane.
so nudging
was never this little.
scrambling this voice
to scream.

...

telling me
i must've lost a glare,
certain little aspects
to gleam,
every bit of worth–
this self-esteem.
holding accountable
while conducting
authoritative dreams.
considerable the pain,
it seems,
scrambling this voice
is all i wanted.

choices

jumping in a bush
of nails pretending
it was a bed of nails.
surrounded by rising fire
of particular colors
through streams
of smoothness,
in the northern lights
feeling trapped.
formally together
in all the brightness,
foretold by the crystal ball
it all then snapped.

...

i didn't want to confront it
so i gave it my all,
exactly all of myself
towards feeling particularly
i don't know, kidnapped?
yet i wasn't truthful
about everything upfront.
so the world i created,
if only cornered-
believed in another's own-
my own riches hunt.

…

the courage i wish, didn't-
wasn't anywhere in sight.
sharing whatever is a penny,
giving my unneeded a thought.
i created long inquiries, this time
i was not actually caught…
to put behind enough
responsibility,
a worry not to obligate…

fancy dinners

maybe, even,
if it was superpowers,
what would i embrace
if i take my helmet off in space?
for a power found within,
so profound simple steps.
maybe i am a superhero?
but hidden underneath a bridge
and holding the silver sword,
the power held me down.
still bestowed,
i didn't even deserve
the crown.

…

how it was handled,
even put down.
everything personal
was… more than
i could ever chew
on a silver platter.
but i was so wrong.
yet worse, i was the one
who waved the silver knives
and flung them
above my head in the air.

...

i was the lunatic
so stay aware.
but at least no one
was hurt.
so definitely everyone
did stay alert
during the silver lining
when i was slicing air.

imminent fire

that blew out
the entire world, it felt.
the same light switch
with such emotional power
talking with my heart,
i felt so gigantic.
but how do i let myself go
of the introductory
villainous era
to prove myself, right?
with such emotional prowess,
when will i finally be…
when i finally fall.

…

so what jump
will finally catch me,
that likely i'm never
that close even
near it at all.
what has my life
even amounted to?
that i needed
the infinite word's
token view?

...

for staying
in the bubble's depiction,
and not even feeling,
it is not even there.
so for some reason
i felt safer
when i am not
breathing
my own air.

is this closure?

how was i hopeless?
losing myself?
learning desperate-
to find myself… again,
in the process.
for dissecting
every daydream,
scattering
the pieces
that once
i blew,

...

then flew
everywhere,
for the version-
that i am today?
trusting-
that who i was
is exactly not
who i am today.
for the deepness
exactly is surface level.

…

except, my brain
by one exact thread,
pulled years away.
feeling so sure,
a new pattern.
i was caught standing
in a watercolor array
of peachy midnight…
only after
the worst storm.

was a vision

i was watching
as if i was someone else.
but i was myself
running around
a hospital bed.
it's weird to be
where it all began:
in a hospital bed.
wrapped in the likely
warm embrace,

…

cradled in the arms
and hands of *the* someone
who brought me into this life.
but later on… passed on
to be adopted
just a bit further down
two years later.
so chasing myself
running around
a hospital bed,
not as myself,
but in a sort of
hallucination like haze,

. . .

on this stage,
i was someone else.
acting as the understudy
for my own life
they put on,
on this stage
watching from
the outside
inside my life.
the peak through
the open seams
as someone else
created the stage

...

of hand picked
scenes in my dreams-
of repression.
i was actually
in this sort of
sleep-like depression.
and i needed
to remember that.

answers

i wanted to connect
all the pieces,
all at once,
in one go:
i, so, was
overwhelmed,
though.
so… have i always
been this sort
of "confident?"
daring, and convinced.

…

never afraid
of the outcome
for the last word,
though?
my voice was heard
during the amazement
of putting up
all the dominoes.
i kept pushing
just never ending
pushing, during

…

the set up
of all of them
falling down,
though.
and from empty air,
there was a balloon
deflated…. finally
in a million
different directions.
when will i catch up
to all of the things
that i have said?

…

to the person
i always think
that i always
have been?
and will be,
for the person
i really think
that i really am…
broken,
in a million pieces.

...

in a way
it resembles
in a million.
one piece is gone.
taken from one
in a million pieces.

living tales of a monster

how come i forget
there's a monster
underneath my bed?
is it living a life
of substantial imagination
with my belongings
while i am sleeping,
haunted over
by the fascination
that i am tossing
and turning in my sleep?
where was i…

…

when it was awake?
the slightest degree
touching,
evermore moving
and removing
my belongings
in my closet?
i left and my closet door
was open again.
it crept out on a trail
with bloody legs, a bloody tail.
with a reflective rainbow
eyes of both horrible intent.

…

sharp as a freshly
scraped fundament.
so how was i…
exactly to describe
what i have seen
when re-entering
my bedroom?
can i just
put it up for rent?
how was it scared
to have a future
with me?
locking eyes,

...

it was mimicking me.
blinking exactly
on the beat.
my heartbeat was scarier
than i could ever imagine.
still there as a thousand-
piece puzzle.
scattered strategically,
scattered in my mind,
a suspects board was
growing.
the investigation
led to a horrendous
unfolding.

...

except, i had every piece
of evidence right in front
of me,
eventually a clue.
eventually i was able
to see through.

Dreaming on the Couch

Finding comfort on
Three exact cushions,
I found solace
In a recurring place.
So grasping these
Certain feelings.
So much of
These feelings,
In another time
Held in wonder
Was shining gold.
Keeping me ahold.

…

Sleepless, for questioning
How everyone
In my household,
Everyone and the sun
Easily fell asleep
During a lifetime ago.
So in my little brain
A lifetime ago I felt
the little turn
Into heavy dangers
Told from thunder
And lightning.

…

I, so much as wanted–
To trail out the front door.
And shout
"what am I so afraid of?"
About rainwater seeping down
My bedroom wall.
Shaking the safety rail
Of my bed,
I shake impossible pain.
Simply the idea
Of drowning in my bedroom.
Drowning me along,
Just simply drowning.
Simply sinking me
All the way down.

implore what i'm found for

the gentle world
that i saw
was the kid
that begun
to see everything
degrade through
a million chances
that began cruel.
so i let go of the world
of make believe,
that when i felt no harm

...

invisible screams
drowned the last touch
of my make-believe dreams.
i slept surrounded.
surrounded dangerous
to say that i finally made it?
that stepping through
finally felt
i was in the dark.
yet hearing the wall
mounted clock focus,

...

i was smearing over
on every tiny little snark
when i couldn't fall back
because i made everything
seem like a question mark.
so sitting on carpet,
the floor strapped.
awakening the buckle,
tried and tighter.
i couldn't retract
or make a peep.
i was focused
on every sheep
counting down

…

from one hundred
and two,
screaming into my pillow
i was trapped.
but i got up,
and i had nowhere to go.
so clearly what i did,
i looked out the window.
finding the whereabouts,
there's still different
parts of the world
i don't know…

somewhere starting adulthood

i think it is wild
how others see the way,
the way that i am.
but how i look inward
is wildly different.
since nature
can be so beautiful-
so cold and natural.
i was above wisdom,
out of body- experiencing
written personality.

...

and exhibiting
soon- studied history.
still, i was writing
and moving history.
it was just as natural
as born given traits.
but growing
into my personality
begun finally,
when i was gone.

...

where i knew- somewhere
i had skeptically led on.
so finally, i just did not care
for what i used to live on.

injured poems

...

it was a haziness feeling.
i walked into my darkened
living room with a shaded figure.
i struggled to find the light
burning my skin and soaking,
melting my mouth from a calling-
so desperately actualizing
this balanced brain power
in believing- morally
the less that i give-
objectively gravitates
to the person i really am.

...

adjusting *almost* every color,
seeing in my own
personal kaleidoscope
staring at the sun,
foolishly and madly
gazing down,
almost noticing any color,
i'd eventually swallow back down
on false memories.
i am looking down
and clenching
my own hands,

...

maybe feeling something?
treating a memory as an ordeal
where learning from it
was nonexistent at the time.
so turning a page
when i- i rewrote
the same thing
over and over again
recreating myself,
so as long as i am
re-interviewing myself.

...

was i actually favored
by the likeness of others?
that emphasizes on-
when i'm battling
my own demons,
it instantly became
too supernatural?
hearing a dangerous voice
harmonizing with insecure-ness
with misdiagnosis for receiving
some sort of medicine.
how have i might
of actually turned out?

...

when i was treated-
i couldn't but more so-
i wouldn't.
wishing i was the one
that got away.
it felt terrifying
to even feel irregular.
with continuous
points of views
telling me i was meant
to be this way.

...

yet contending the thought
of actually being irregular
was practically manic
when i really didn't know.
and sitting high as a king,
i sat high on a throne.
i had an entire view,
an aerial view.
except- the higher
i felt on an already
almost crumbling
half supported

...

black wooden chair,
pilled two or more
phone books,
i placed a house
of cards.
i kept building
the walls stronger.
and inside was
an entire built
civilization with a king
and a queen.
i crafted the perfect
piece of an invasion.

...

so what color was i
feeling when i see
a house burning down?
for rain trickling like gasoline,
when the reflection of fire met
in an otherworldly space.
i stuck a guitar string
in an electrical outlet
and i saw the smoke rise,
and instantly my eyes
became just mesmerized
by the little things.

…

putting pressure
on the perfect picture
for the darker blue
of standing on my own
to feel…
detrimental
and actually
comprehending regret.
about- beginning
to truly comprehend
this regret.

. . .

because when
my youth disappeared,
my inner world felt
amazingly dark
most of the time.
so not handing over
this power
in the beginning-
failing when staring-
at this younger version
only made an evil
appearance lather
in every changing costume.

...

the scared little boy
afraid of the dark
was meant.

a step into

some other time i let go:

Mystery Edition

Coming this Fall

sensational

pieces of my childhood
were still emerging,
the vigilance to reflect
is never concluded.
so further in my life,
i have claimed
feeling lost…
but, lately i want
to feel safe.
so the nail i picture
is safely put in.
the nail, as a pretty penny.
but, imagine the nail,
not what it seemed.
inverted- pounding halfway.
only quite forces
were at play.

. . .

how did i act out a scenario
i say to portray,
an image i wanted
to vicariously throw away.
reaching…
seeing way more
than i ever should.
a dangerous game to say.
so could my world
be slowly
slipping backwards
into a familiar place?
i felt sensational.
feeling captivated now,
when at the time
i felt ignorant.

…

i was sensational to feel
a sentiment flying an invitation
from all around the world
that only i got to open.

my brain cover

it's nothing…
i'd hate to say-
or *"stop"*
or wait-
it's not
what i imagined…
standing alone-
ashamed i was
nice enough to myself?
please leave- and
never come back
is pure darkness.
so i see a stranger
walking closer
at a slower pace,

...

though i cannot
find a decryption.
i'll just walk on over.
so i take any part
of my brain
and open my braincase:
but that's illogical.
and utterly crush it into pieces
because likely i'll just
have to keep it brief.
and any detail
i'll just have to
delicately erase
since blocked
in hidden space,

...

a shooting star
had slipped so slightly
with grace.
though, which space
was i talking about?
walking alone-
brushed- feverish
with termination darkness,
walking alone surrounded
in a hint of purple,
i think i've lived
this life before.
where tortured souls are
there could be werewolves?

...

but that's the craziest thing
told by far.
ironically it was
full that night.
"oh, i meant to say
a full moon.
a yellow-ish pasty
dried pastel moon
washed away
The Fearful Night Sky,
capable- wringing out
color-
painted uneasily uneven
harsh too unsynchronized

...

full of bright speckled stars,
darkness with a hint of purple.
ironically it was the flashing light
from a passing helicopter.
in fact- that night
i saw many bright
speckled stars.
so does it happen every night?
all during a full moon,
is everything flooded,
blinded- flushed by an off-white?
when late night thinking
became a brand new height.

…

bringing out the worst
condition of thinking?
so am i right?
the scenic route of
directions hover a skylight
way in thinking?

unspoken narrative

phantom wildfire

i felt the unknown
territory,
the universe took
a gigantic leap
because i found you.
the takeoff
for falling in love
when both
of our minds
i thought-
collided.
but after
i poured
my feelings,

...

i shattered
how i really felt.
because when
you asked
i still felt
not okay to say
my internal temperature
just started to melt.
so when i took a stand
i objected that i was okay,
it was difficult to say-
fairly so
i'm falling for you.

...

and it was
not slightly reciprocated
in any direct way.
blinded by a connection
you felt entirely different
inviting me out to dinner.
our intimate wording
of a deep connection,
i took it as a green lit sign.
you didn't see me
that night- the same.

…

but our immediate
eye contact
threw us off
our friendship
when i felt
the feelings,
you kept reassuring
"are you okay?"
when you didn't
feel the same.

About the Author

Born in Ukraine and raised in Florida, Daniel was adopted at the age of just a mere two years old. He couldn't even imagine what life may have in store for him. Daniel S. Sandorf's debut book is finally here. He hadn't really found his passion for poetry just until four years ago. During those years he spent finding his writing voice. What was his perspective on? What makes Daniel who he is? He knew from an early age he had a creative mind, yet what could he do with an overactive brain? One creative outlet being, during childhood, one of his favorite video games was Minecraft. It strengthened, and even tested his limits. The possibilities he wandered about. The only reference was the use of his imagination. He saw it in his own unique lens just like his writing. A different perspective on things. In his debut book, he created a narrative that even surprised him. The emotion and even depth, how he became capable of unlocking stored memories. Creating was his call to action. He's still pretty fresh in the world of writing. He is still learning about the qualities of what makes a great writer.

Acknowledgements

It's crazy how this book became something. Idea after idea, even I don't know how it happened. It's difficult to wrap my head around such an idea that I wrote a book?? I want to thank two of my closest friends who stood by my side through it all. Jessica and Ayonna. Thank you, Jessica, for the constructive criticism, even when I did not accept it or called you some harsh things. You *like* made my writing *like* better. You are a main contributor to why I revamped my entire writing style. Thank you, Ayonna for being my photographer and capturing an unforgettable moment. Some of our late night conversations influenced two poems I wrote.

misunderstanding, poem that you named. And *out there,* the beginning line you inspired me to write. Thank you to everyone who I had deep meaningful interactions with. There's a 99% chance that I wrote about it and turned it into writing material.

www.ingramcontent.com/pod-product-compliance
Lightning Source LLC
La Vergne TN
LVHW090515110826
845146LV00003B/873

* 9 7 9 8 2 1 8 3 7 8 3 0 1 *